# Pope
# John Paul II
# Pope for the People

Peggy Burns

HODDER
*Wayland*

an imprint of Hodder Children's Books

Produced for Hodder Wayland by
Roger Coote Publishing
Gissing's Farm, Fressingfield
Suffolk IP21 5SH, UK

**Title page: The Pope with Mother Teresa of Calcutta**

Project Manager: Alex Edmonds
Designer: Tessa Barwick
Cover designer: Ian Kaye
Indexer: Caroline Hamilton

Published in Great Britain in 2000 by Hodder Wayland,
an imprint of Hodder Children's Books

A Catalogue record for this book is available from the
British Library.

ISBN 07502 2823 7

Printed and bound in Italy by
G. Canale & C.S.p.A., Turin

Hodder Children's Books
A division of Hodder Headline Limited
338 Euston Road, London NW1 3BH

**Picture Acknowledgements**
The publishers would like to thank the following
for allowing their pictures to be reproduced in this
publication: Corbis Images 6; Getty Images 4, 7,
13, 14, 16, 24; Rex Features 1, 5, 8, 9, 10, 11, 12,
17, 18, 19, 20, 21, 22, 23, 25, 26, 27, 28, 31, 32,
34, 35, 36, 37, 38, 39, 40, 41, 42, 43, 45;
Topham Picturepoint 15, 29, 30, 33, 44.

While every effort has been made to secure
permission, in some cases it has proved impossible
to trace copyright holders.

# Contents

# White Smoke

*Crowds of people waited outside the Vatican for hours, eager to know who the new Pope was.*

It was 16 October 1978, and in St Peter's Square in Rome, Italy, the evening air was filled with excitement. More than a hundred thousand people watched and waited; high above their heads, brilliant lights lit the chimney of the Vatican palace, and every eye was fixed on the famous rooftop.

*The first Polish Pope delighted the people when he spoke to them from the balcony in fluent Italian.*

Suddenly, white smoke billowed from the chimney. The smoke was white instead of black – a special signal which told the waiting crowd that a new Pope had been chosen.

Now, everybody wanted to know who he was! The people pressed eagerly forward as someone stepped out on to the balcony to tell them the new Pope's name. The cardinals had voted for Karol Wojtyla, who was Polish. There was a gasp of surprise from the crowd, as they had never had a Polish Pope before. In fact, for the last 456 years every Pope had been Italian! Everyone broke into loud cheers.

# Choosing a Name

The last Pope had been John Paul I, and he had died after being Pope for only 33 days. It was the custom for each new Pope to choose a name for himself, and Karol Wojtyla decided that in the previous Pope's memory he would be called John Paul II. New popes usually choose the name of a previous pope whose teachings they admire. At 58, he was the youngest Pope for more than 100 years.

*After John Paul I's death, the Cardinals prepared to be locked away inside the Vatican, where they would once more vote in secret for a new Pope.*

John Paul II was now the leader of the Roman Catholic church – more than 700 million people around the world. Roman Catholics, who are part of the Christian church, follow the teachings of Jesus Christ.

In the early evening of October 16, 1978, the great crowd in St Peter's Square stirred as Pope John Paul II walked on to the balcony of the Vatican palace to greet his people for the first time. Most of them were Italian, and they wondered if the Pope could speak Italian – or would he speak to them in Polish?

*The newly-elected John Paul II put on the special cassock and headdress – known as a mitre – and said Mass for the first time as Pope.*

# Dancing in the Streets

The people need not have worried. John Paul II, in fact, could not only speak Italian, but English, German, Spanish, French and Russian as well! When he spoke to them in their own language, the crowd broke into loud cheering. Everyone was very relieved.

Catholics all over the world were thrilled when they heard that their new Pope was Polish. Most Polish people are Roman Catholics, though their Government frowned on the Christian faith. They made life difficult for people who believed in God.

*Karol – the future Pope – was 13 when he took communion for the first time. Even as a child his Christian faith took first place in his life.*

*The people clapped and cheered as the new Pope blessed them in the name of God the Father, the Son and the Holy Spirit.*

It was beyond their wildest dreams to have a Polish Pope, and they were overjoyed when they heard the wonderful news. John Paul II had grown up among them. They knew and loved this very special man – and now he was the greatest Christian leader in the world. In the streets, complete strangers hugged each other and cried with joy. Waving flags and banners they crowded into the parks, laughing and singing.

*On his first day as Pope, John Paul II visited a friend in hospital. In the corridors, crowds waited, hoping to catch a glimpse of him as he passed. He had to be reminded that he should bless the people with the sign of the cross. He did so with a smile. "I'm not used to it yet," he told them.*

# A Boy and his Father

The people of Poland were very proud of John Paul II; many of them knew him well and older people remembered him as a little boy. Karol was born on May 18, 1920. He came from a very ordinary family. He and his parents and older brother Edmund lived in a small flat. His father, a retired army lieutenant, suffered from ill health and had retired with only a small pension. Karol's mother sewed for friends and neighbours to make a little extra money. Sadly, she died when Karol was still a small boy. Four years later Edmund also died, and Karol and his father were left alone.

*Karol's parents wanted him to become a priest. "My Lolek [his nickname] will grow up to be a great man," his mother often told the neighbours.*

Karol (second from left), pictured with his parish priest, Father Fidusiewicz, and a group of choirboys from the church he attended in Wadowice, his home town.

## The football-crazy brothers

*"His brother Edmund was a medical student then. He used to take Karol to football matches, carrying him on his shoulders so that he could see better."*
An older friend.

The boy and his father went for long walks together. As they walked they talked a lot, especially about the Christian faith, and Karol grew to love God. Every morning on his way to school he would go to church to pray.

11

# The World is about to Change

Although his faith took the first place in his life, Karol found that there were many other things to enjoy.

He was clever, and he enjoyed school. But his great love was sport. Canoeing, skiing, mountaineering, swimming – he loved them all. It was football, though, that was his favourite game, and he was happiest when playing in goal.

*A keen sportsman and athlete, Karol enjoyed cycling and walking in the countryside.*

**Adolf Hitler, leader of the Nazi Party, invaded Poland on September 1, 1939, sparking off the Second World War.**

When he was 18, Karol left school and went on to the university in Crakow, where he studied the Polish language, literature and poetry. Soon, he began to write poetry himself. A warm and friendly person, Karol found it easy to make friends. He joined a drama group and discovered that he loved acting even more than he loved saving goals. He passed all his exams with flying colours in the summer of 1939. Life was good. But for how long? Things were about to change, not just for Karol, but for all Poland...

*One of Karol's first poems shows us how much he still missed his mother. He called it The White Grave:*

*Over Your white grave*
*White flowers of life bloom –*
*Oh, how many years have gone by*
*Without You – how many years?...*
*Over Your white grave*
*O Mother, my extinct beloved,*
*For a son's full love,*
*A prayer: Eternal Rest.*

# Terrible Times

Across Europe, people were beginning to fear Adolf Hitler, the Chancellor of Germany. Hitler saw himself and his Nazi party as having absolute power, not only in Germany but across Europe.

He took over Austria, then attacked Czechoslovakia. In September 1939, Hitler invaded Poland, and the Second World War began. Under Nazi rule everything changed. Life in Poland became a nightmare for ordinary people.

*Adolf Hitler became Chancellor in 1933. He dreamed of creating a huge empire that would last for a thousand years.*

*In September 1939 German troops marched into Poland. Within a few weeks, Poland surrendered to the Nazis.*

Thousands were sent to prison camps, where they died or were killed. Food was scarce, and people went hungry. When they could get bread it often contained wood shavings.

Hitler wanted to destroy the Catholic church, and hundreds of priests were imprisoned. Nearly 2,000 Catholic priests died during the war. Hitler also closed the universities and upper schools, and imprisoned many university tutors – he was afraid that educated people would challenge his rule. Every Polish adult was forced to do hard labour.

*What Adolf Hitler thought about Polish people:*
*"The Poles are especially born for low labour. It is necessary to keep the standard of life low in Poland, and it must not be permitted to rise."*
Adolf Hitler.

15

# Secret Studies

Outwardly, this arrangement appeared to be working. But education went underground...

University professors and teachers bravely arranged secret classes in the cellars of private homes. Students – including Karol – were able to carry on studying, and even take exams, at the "underground university". Karol studied the Bible, the Catholic faith, history and Latin.

*Many thousands of Polish Jews were rounded up and taken to the death camp at Auschwitz.*

Then in 1940 Karol got a job in a quarry, breaking up huge stones with a heavy hammer. It was backbreaking work. But Karol believed that hard work gave people self respect, and he worked hard and did the very best job he could.

*Karol (circled), and other actors in Cracow. They performed plays secretly in private homes.*

**How a fellow worker saw Karol:**
**"On the night shift, at about twelve o'clock he would kneel on the factory floor and say his prayers. Not all the other workers took kindly to this — some of them used to tease him by throwing things."**

Before long, he was given a better job in the Solway Factory, near Cracow. Life was still hard, but his religion, his good friends, and his love of the theatre kept him going.

Hitler had banned live theatre, and many actors were arrested and sent to prison camps. But Karol risked the danger and joined a small drama group which staged secret performances.

17

# Loneliness

More sadness and suffering lay in store for Karol.

Unexpectedly, his beloved father died. The young man was devastated; he was only 21 years old, and he had no close family left. He sat by his father's body all night, thinking and praying and grieving for his father. God seemed very close to him, and it crossed his mind that God could be calling him to be a priest. But he dismissed the thought, as he had already made up his mind that one day he would be a great actor.

*"Karol prayed a little, then he talked a little with me about life and death," wrote a friend who sat with him when his father died. It was a turning point in Karol's life.*

Not long after his father's death, Karol was knocked down by a tram and was badly hurt. The young man became convinced that there was some deep reason behind these experiences. More than ever, he felt that he was being called to spend his life serving God. But he knew that if he became a priest his life would never be the same again.

*The Pope at prayer. All his life John Paul II has believed that prayer and faith in God are the only real weapons against evil.*

# A Life-changing Decision

As a priest, Karol would have to forget his dreams of becoming an actor. And, as Roman Catholic priests are not allowed to marry, he would never have a wife, or be the father of a family.

It was a decision that would change his life, and he thought about it for a long time, praying that God would show him the right way. Finally, his mind was made up: he would be a priest. The church would be his family, and he would be a father to the people who lived around him. In 1942 he started studying for the priesthood at the secret university.

*Though the Pope has no children of his own, he has always had a genuine love of children and believes strongly in family life.*

Meanwhile the fighting went on, but by the beginning of 1945, Germany was losing the war. In January 1945, Russian soldiers marched in to free Poland from Germany's rule, and for the first time in six years people felt free again. They hoped that their lives would quickly get back to normal.

Karol's workmates tried to find him a girlfriend:
"We didn't know in those days that he was going to be a priest, and we once tried to introduce him to a girl, but he wasn't having any. He didn't make a fuss, just ignored the subject."
Jozef Krasuski, a worker at the Solway factory.

21

# A Priest – at Last

At last Karol was free to attend university openly. In the summer of 1945, he took his final examinations, and his results were amazing. In 19 of his 26 exams he achieved the highest possible marks – and he only lost one mark in six of his other subjects!

Watched by his many friends, Karol was ordained as a priest on November 1, 1946. He was 26 years old, and it was clear to the church authorities that there was something special about this outstanding student. They sent him to study in Rome for another two years.

*Karol's exam results put him near the top of his class. He was ordained six months ahead of his classmates.*

Once there, Karol worked very hard, and two years later, in 1950, he became a Doctor of Divinity. Soon after that he went back home to Poland. But conditions in Poland were still bad. The country now had a Communist government, who were very much against the Christian church. The university's department of theology, where Karol had studied, was once more closed down.

Karol's many friends missed him very much when he left Poland for Rome, where he continued with his studies.

# A Generous Heart

The new government was determined to stamp out religion, and some priests were sent to prison camps. Schools were forbidden to teach religion, and many Catholic organisations were banned.

In July 1948, Karol went to work in a village church in Niegowic, and the people took him to their hearts. He lived a very simple life. He owned very few things, and his clothes were shabby, but all the same, he was generous. Some said he was too generous. When villagers found out that he slept on the floor, they bought him some bedding – which he later gave to a woman who had been robbed! It was a sad day for the village when he moved on to St Florian's, a bigger church in Cracow.

*Father Karol shaves in the open air. The young priest often took parties of young men and women on long mountain walks.*

*Karol kept in touch with people from all walks of life.*

People began to talk about Karol and his unusual message that people could grow nearer to God if they stopped trying to get rich and were content with what they had.

*However uncomfortable he was, Karol always put his people before himself. Visiting them in their homes was particularly bad in the winter. He told a friend: "Snow will cling to your cassock, then it will thaw out indoors, and freeze again outside, forming a heavy bell around your legs, which gets heavier and heavier... By evening, you could hardly drag your legs. But you have to go on, because you know that people wait for you."*

# The Cardinal who Cared

People could see that their priest, who went around dressed in well-worn clothes, practised what he preached, and every Sunday crowds packed into St Florian's to hear his sermons.

Soon after moving to St Florian's Karol started up a youth group, mainly to teach children about the Christian faith. But his Christianity covered every part of life, and the boys loved it when he took the time to play football with them on the common.

*Karol became known as the Cardinal who really cared about people. He set aside time every day for anyone who wanted to talk with him.*

It was soon time for Karol to move on again, and once more he went back to his studies. The brilliant young man gained one qualification after another, progressing steadily in the church. In June 1967, at the very young age of 47, he was made a cardinal – the most important position in the Roman Catholic church except that of Pope.

But however important he became, Karol never lost touch with ordinary people, and he never forgot that millions around the world were suffering.

*It was a special day for the people of Wadowice when Cardinal Karol Wojtyla visited his home town.*

# Gentle Persuasion

It saddened Karol to know of the terrible conditions in which so many people had to live, especially those in poor, Third-world countries. In places where there was fighting, many had been driven from their homes, left to starve, tortured and even killed. Warm-hearted and caring by nature, Karol longed to be able to do something to help — but he knew that those countries' leaders would have to change before life could improve for ordinary people.

*Bill Clinton, the U.S. President, is just one of the world leaders the Pope has met and talked with.*

*The prayers, the teaching and the love of Pope John Paul II touches the lives of ordinary people.*

And then, in 1978, he became Pope John Paul II. As the most important religious leader in the world, he was now free to talk to the rulers of those countries where people were suffering. He could gently persuade those who were fighting to talk instead of killing each other. He could sympathise with poor and needy people, and condemn the rich who cared about nobody but themselves. Perhaps Karol could now begin to make a real difference in their lives.

*The Pope was always outraged when innocent people were killed, and he often preached on the subject. "God once said, 'Don't kill!' Man... any group of men... can't change and trample this most sacred law of God! Those who have on their consciences the weight of so many human victims, must understand... that they can't be allowed to kill innocents. I say to those responsible, 'Repent!' One day the judgment of God will come!"*

# The Pope who Loves People

The new Pope lived a very busy life, writing speeches, conducting services and reading countless letters. But he made sure that he still met ordinary people. He set up a "General Audience" every Wednesday; large crowds would gather in St Peter's Square to see him, and he would move slowly among them in his white jeep (the Popemobile), shaking hands and chatting to them.

*A Christmas Day blessing from Pope John Paul II in December 1996 – in 55 different languages!*

Three months after he was elected, the Pope visited Mexico, where huge crowds lined the streets to welcome him. It was to be the first of many foreign tours, and around the world people began to love and respect him. Wherever he went, whether he was visiting a children's hospital or talking to factory workers, people gathered in their thousands to hear him speak and receive his blessing. In June 1979, the Polish government allowed John Paul II to visit his homeland for the first time as Pope.

*The Pope carries on working for peace, dignity and freedom of humankind.*

*Ginka Beer was an old friend from the Pope's childhood. When she visited Rome many years later, John Paul II recognised her among the crowd in St Peter's Square. Ginka told him that her father had been killed in Russia, and her mother had died. "He just looked at me," she said afterwards, "and there was deep compassion in his eyes... He took both my hands and for almost two minutes he blessed me and prayed."*

# The Pope Returns to Poland

John Paul II had come home, and in Poland, vast crowds turned out to welcome him. For the first time, a Pope was visiting a country ruled by a Communist government, and it was a great occasion. Everywhere he went, thousands of people gathered. Church bells rang out joyfully as he arrived in the capital, Warsaw.

**The Polish Government tried to stamp out the Christian faith. But the people showed their faith when the Pope visited Poland.**

But no trip to Poland would be complete without visiting Cracow, where he had worked and studied during the war. He travelled there by helicopter, and as he arrived he saw, spread out below, an immense sea of people. It was an unbelievable sight – more than a million people had gathered to greet him! As he stepped from the helicopter he shouted, "I'm back, my children!" – and a great roar went up from the crowd.

His tour, as well as being one of great joy, also had its sadness. There was one visit that the Pope could not leave Poland without making...

# The Pope sees for Himself

As a young man during the war, the Pope had often seen people beaten up, arrested, and sent off to prison camp. Thousands of them – some of them his friends – had been loaded like cattle on to railway trucks and taken to the dreaded death camp at Auschwitz. In the camp, two million people had been murdered and their bodies burnt. Now, the Pope felt that he needed to see Auschwitz for himself.

At a wooden altar set up between the railway lines that had seen trainloads of people brought to the camp, he prayed for those who had died there so long ago, and celebrated Mass.

*During the war, some of the Pope's own friends had died in the gas chambers at Auschwitz.*

*Many ex-prisoners who had survived the death camp returned to Auschwitz to hear the Pope's message.*

Before he left Poland, John Paul II visited Wadowice, where he had lived as a boy, and the whole town turned out to welcome him back. He was thrilled to meet again the parish priest who was his teacher for six years.

The Pope's visit to Poland had been a huge success.

# John Paul II – we want you!

The Pope's foreign tours continued, and everywhere he preached his message of peace and God's love.

In September and October 1979, he visited Ireland and the USA. In Ireland, Catholics and Protestants had been fighting each other for many years. John Paul II begged both sides to put hatred and violence behind them and make friends. From Ireland he went on to the USA, where he became the first Pope to visit the president, at that time Jimmy Carter, in the White House.

*President Jimmy Carter welcomed John Paul II as a messenger of peace. American children showered the Pope with gifts – among them a guitar and a pair of jeans!*

*In Ireland the Pope begged people to turn away from violence and live in peace with each other.*

Every radio and TV channel teemed with news about the Pope, and it seemed that everybody, from the President to people living in the poorest districts of New York, fell under his spell. "Pope John Paul II – we want you!" the crowds chanted – and were delighted with his reply: "Pope John Paul II – I want you!"

In his nine-day trip John Paul II travelled 10,000 miles and preached 72 sermons, sleeping for only around four and a half hours a night.

# "I will kill the Pope!"

The Pope had become a well-known and well-loved figure around the world. But not everybody loved him. A man who spoke up so boldly for the poor and oppressed was bound to gain some enemies!

One of his enemies was Mehmet Ali Agca, a criminal in a top security prison in Turkey. In 1979 Agca escaped – then boldly wrote to a newspaper stating that he was going to kill the Pope! The police hunted far and wide, but there was no trace of Agca. When they heard that he had entered Italy using a fake passport, the Italian police searched desperately – but Agca had disappeared.

*As the Pope greets people in the crowd, Mehmet Ali Agca raises a gun and fires several shots.*

*The Pope's secretary caught him as he fell, gravely injured. Two women were also injured in the attack.*

For John Paul II, May 13, 1981 was like any other normal day. Riding in his white jeep, the Pope was smiling affectionately, waving to groups of children, exchanging a few words with people as usual. Then without warning a series of shots rang out across St Peter's Square...

# The World Waits

Clutching a bullet wound in his chest, John Paul II staggered and fell. As they realised that he had been shot, the people around him were stunned. They could not believe that anyone would try to kill their beloved leader. Within minutes the Pope was in an ambulance and on his way to hospital.

*The Pope's injuries were serious. A bullet wounded him in the stomach and missed his heart by millimetres.*

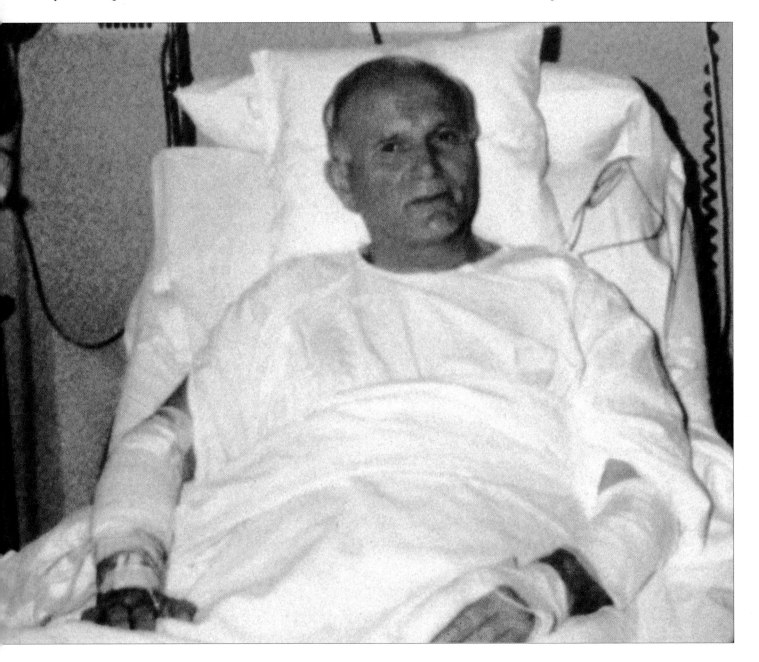

**Silent and anxious, people gather in St Peter's Square to wait for news.**

In the Pope's own words: "I wish to address my thanks – my special thanks – to the young of the whole world, who have been particularly close to me in this period of suffering with their affection and their prayers. Let them rest assured that their messages and their prayers have really been a support and comfort to me."

He was badly injured, and in an operation that lasted five hours doctors fought to save his life. Around the world people waited anxiously by their radios and TV sets. Would the Pope live – or die? At 10.30 that night came the news they had prayed for; John Paul II would pull through. Typically, as soon as he was able, he told everyone that he had forgiven Agca.

But it was to be some time before the Pope was really on the road to recovery. Three weeks later, infection set in and he had to return to hospital for another operation.

41

# Love your Enemies

Once he was fit to go back to work, John Paul II was soon as busy as ever. In 1983 he visited Ali Agca, his would-be murderer, in prison. The Pope firmly believed in the teaching of Jesus Christ, who told his followers, "Love your enemies", so we can be sure that John Paul II told Agca that he forgave him for trying to kill him.

We can only guess at why Agca tried to kill the Pope. Some believe it was a Communist plot, while others think it was for religious reasons.

*The Russian leader, Mikhail Gorbachev, believed that the Pope was responsible for the improved relationships between many countries.*
*"Everything that happened in Eastern Europe in these last few years would have been impossible without the presence of this Pope and without the important role – including the political role – that he played on the world stage."*

*The Pope forgives the man who tried to kill him. Before John Paul II left Agca's prison cell, the would-be assassin knelt and kissed his hand.*

*Pope John Paul II with Mother Teresa of Calcutta – a woman known across the world for her care and compassion for people in need.*

The attempt on his life did not stop the Pope speaking out for peace, and in the coming years he was to meet many powerful world leaders.

His message to them was not based on politics, but on compassion for anyone who was suffering. He had no interest in taking their land or ruling their countries, but simply in persuading them to respect the rights of other people.

# Hope for the World

By the mid 1990s, Pope John Paul II had taken more than 40 foreign tours, and his message of love and hope made a great impression on powerful men around the world. Leaders from Middle Eastern countries which had been at war for many years; presidents from the United States; Mikhail Gorbachev, the Russian President; Lech Walesa of Poland; Fidel Castro of Cuba; Nelson Mandela of South Africa — all met the Pope, and many agreed to work together towards peace. Even those who disagreed with him on many issues admitted that he was a great influence for good.

*Nelson Mandela, the former South African leader, gives the Pope a warm welcome as he arrives in South Africa.*

Human rights have always been of vital concern to the Pope. In Cuba he and the leader, Fidel Castro, had much to talk about.

A newspaper reporter's view: "The Pope is the one person who can be called a world leader... It does not appear to be a role he has set out to fill but people have almost forced it upon him. They sense his goodness and selflessness." Rowanne Pascoe, Editor of *The Universe*.

As the new millennium dawned in 2000, the Pope was 80 years old. Like many older people, his body is weaker and stooped with age. But John Paul II continues to preach his simple message: the call for all nations to lay down their weapons and live in peace.

# Glossary

**Benign tumour** A lump or growth in the body that is harmless, but is often initially suspected to be cancerous.

**Cardinal** A leader in the Roman Catholic church.

**Communist government** A government made up of members of the Communist party – a political system which does not believe in God.

**Invade** To attack another country.

**Literature** Books and texts.

**Mass** A special Roman Catholic service held to remember Christ's important last meal of bread and wine.

**Nazi Party** The National Socialist German Workers' Party who came to power in Germany under Adolf Hitler.

**Ordained** When someone is made a priest.

**Politics** The way a country is governed.

**Pope** The head of the Roman Catholic church.

**Pray** To talk with God.

**Protestants** A Christian who does not belong to the Roman Catholic or Orthodox churches.

**Quarry** A place where stone is dug out of the ground.

**Theology** The study of the Christian religion.

**University** A college of further education where people study to gain a degree.

**Vatican** A large palace in Rome where the Pope lives.

# Further Reading

**His Holiness Pope John Paul II**: Joan Collins, Ladybird Books 1982.
**Christians Through the Ages: Around the World**: John Drane, Lion Publishing 1994.
**I am a Roman Catholic – My Belief**: Brenda Pettenuzzo, Watts Books 1985.

# Websites

http://www.vatican.va/ – the official Vatican web site
http://www.zpub.com/un/pope/ – the unofficial Pope John Paul II website
http://www.pbs.org/wgbh/pages/frontline/shows/pope/ – John Paul II: the millennial pope
http://www.catholic.net/RCC/POPE/Pope.html – His Holiness John Paul II

# Date Chart

**May 18, 1920**  Karol Josef Wojtyla is born in Wadowice, near Cracow, in Poland.

**April 1, 1929**  Karol's mother, Emilia Wojtyla, dies at the age of 45 from heart and kidney problems. Karol is just eight years old.

**December 5, 1932**  Karol's brother, Edmund, a doctor, dies from scarlet fever, a disease he caught from a patient.

**June 1938**  Karol enrols as a student of Polish Philosophy at Jagiellonian University in Cracow.

**September 1, 1939**  The Second World War begins, and Adolf Hitler invades Poland.

**November 1, 1940**  Karol Wojtyla goes to work as a stone cutter in a quarry.

**February 18, 1941**  Karol's father – also called Karol – dies from heart attack. Karol keeps watch all night over his father's body.

**October 1942**  Wojtyla begins studying for the priesthood at the "underground university".

**February 19, 1944**  Wojtyla is hit by a truck and is badly injured. His is taken to hospital with serious head wounds.

**November 1, 1946** At the age of 26, Karol Wojtyla is ordained a priest.

**July 1948** Father Wojtyla is given his first position as curate in the village of Niegowic.

**August 1949**  Father Wojtyla is moved to St Florians, a bigger church in Cracow.

**June 28, 1967**  Wojtyla is made a cardinal by Pope Paul VI.

**September 19, 1978**  At the age of 66, and after only 33 days as Pope, John Paul I dies.

**October 16, 1978**  Cardinal Karol Wojtyla is elected as the new Pope. The first-ever Polish Pope, he chooses to be known as Pope John Paul II.

**June 2, 1979** John Paul II visits Poland for the first time as Pope.

**September 1979**  Pope John Paul II visits Ireland, where he begs Protestants and Catholics to make peace with each other.

**October 1979** Pope John Paul II visits the USA, where he meets the President, Jimmy Carter.

**May 13, 1981** Mehmet Ali Agca, a Turkish man, shoots the Pope.

**May 17, 1981** From his hospital bed, the Pope publicly forgives Agca.

**December 27, 1983** The Pope visits Mehmet Ali Agca in the Rebibbia prison.

**July 12, 1992** John Paul II goes to hospital for tests. Three days later he has an operation to remove a benign tumour.

**November 11, 1993** The Pope dislocates his right shoulder in a fall at the Vatican.

**January 3, 1998** After an earthquake in Italy, the Pope visits the victims.

**January 2000** As the new millennium begins, Pope John Paul II begins his 80th year.

# Index

All numbers in **bold** refer to pictures as well as text.